Fairy and Fantasy 2
Grayscale Coloring Book
by Christine Karron

FAIRY and FANTASY 2
Grayscale Coloring book by Christine Karron

First published January 2021

Copyright 2021 Christine Karron
All rights reserved

Other than for personal use or book review, no part of this book may be reproduced or transmitted in any form or by any means, electronic or mechanical, recording or by any information storage and retrieval system, without written permission from the copyright holder.

ISBN: 9798591923891
Imprint: Independently published

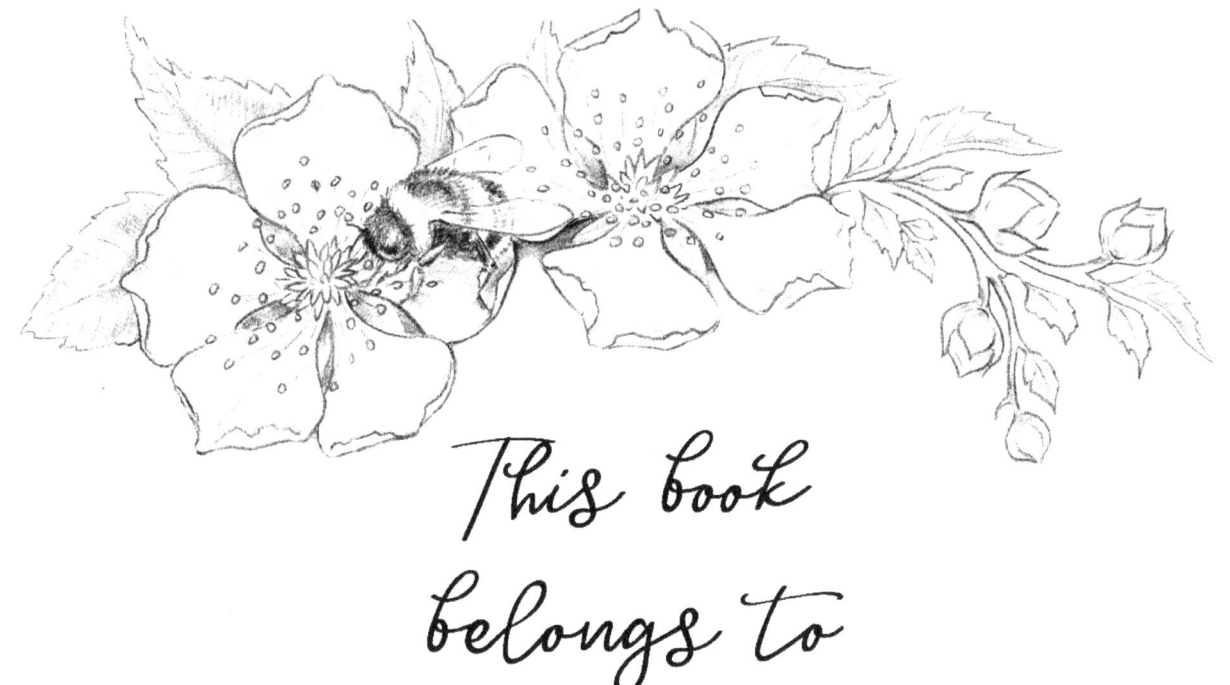

This book belongs to

....

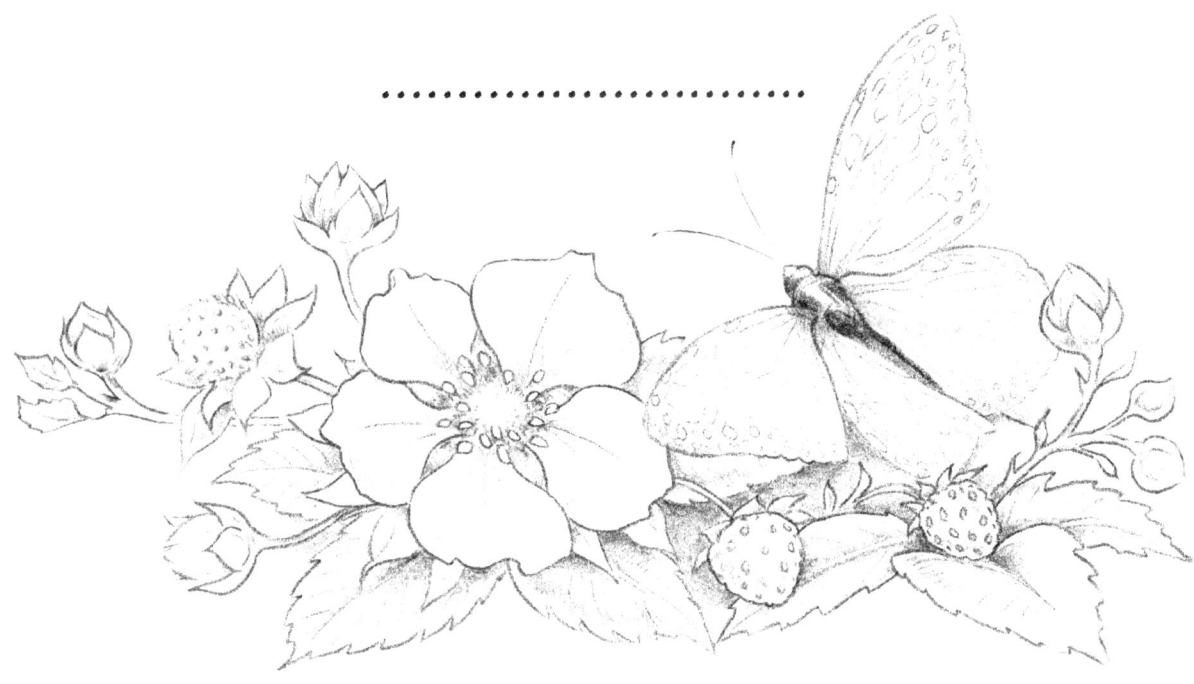

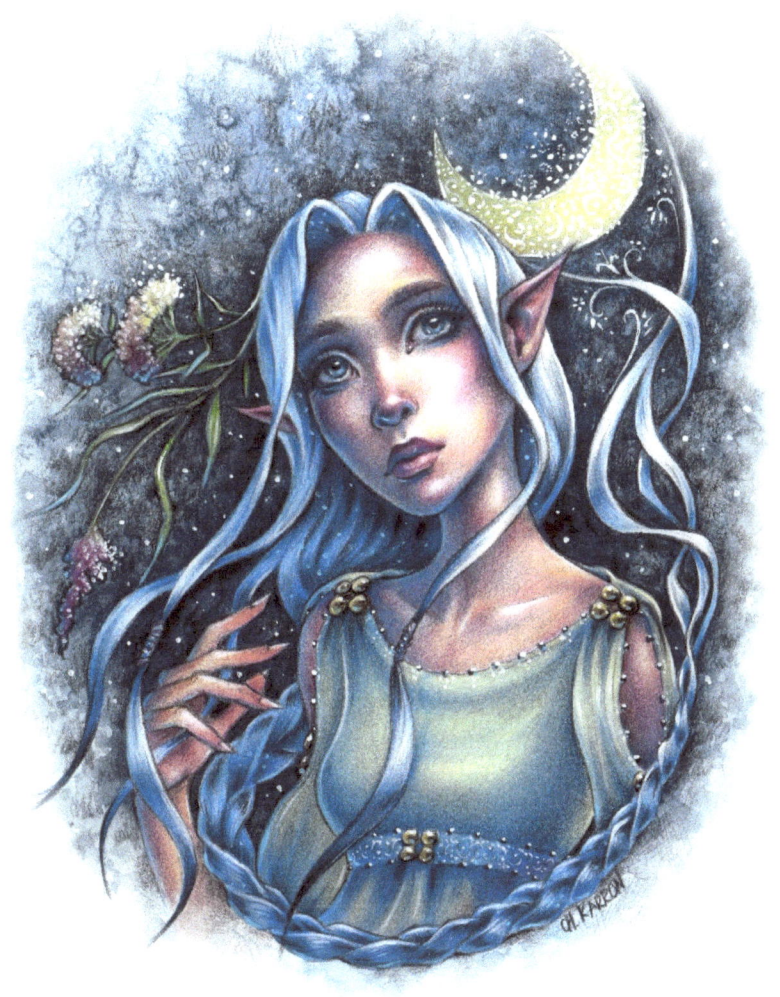

All illustrations in this book were originally created and traditionally hand drawn by the artist Christine Karron. For coloring inspirations, demo videos and more about Christine's artwork visit www.chkarron.com

This coloring book is designed for experienced colorists and beginners as well. Recommended for coloring with markers, colored pencils, pens and/or crayons. If using wet media, place a sheet of thick paper or card stock behind the coloring page to prevent bleed through.

Fairy and Fantasy 2

1. Sugarplum Fairy
2. Hydrangea
3. Little Red Riding Hood
4. Summer Night Fiddler
5. Transience
6. Beloved
7. Ocean Eyes
8. Midnight Enchantress
9. Wildberry Bloom
10. Queen's Chalice
11. Angel Eyes
12. Wood Elfling
13. Forest Song
14. While Sunflowers Bloom
15. Leaf Rider
16. Last Harvest
17. Lady Witch
18. Small Wonders
19. Dark Eyes
20. Fallen

Bonus

21. Cup Of Warmth
22. Sweet Temptation
23. Polar Bear's Comfy Evening
24. Australia

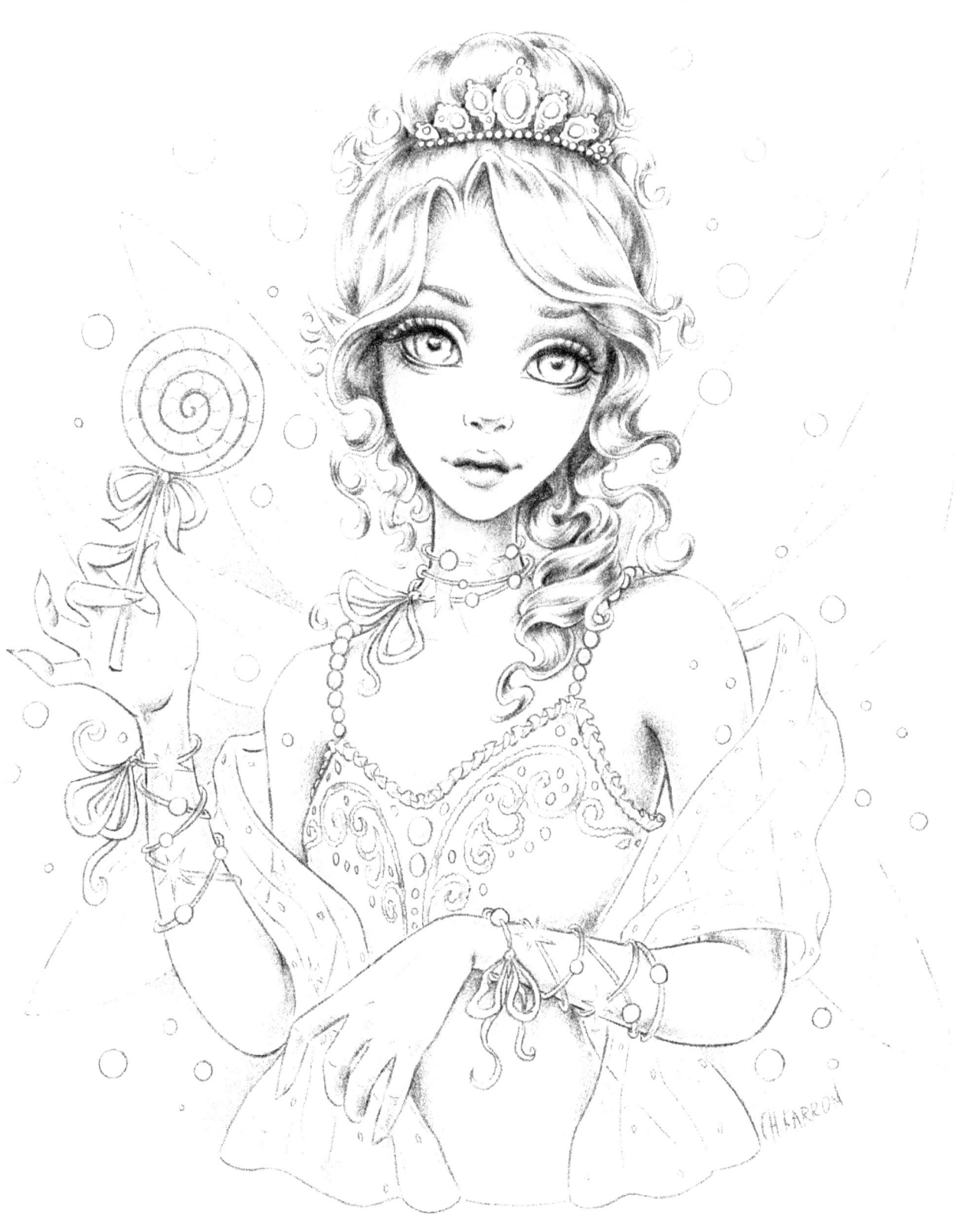

Fairy and Fantasy 2 © Christine Karron — Sugar Plum Fairy

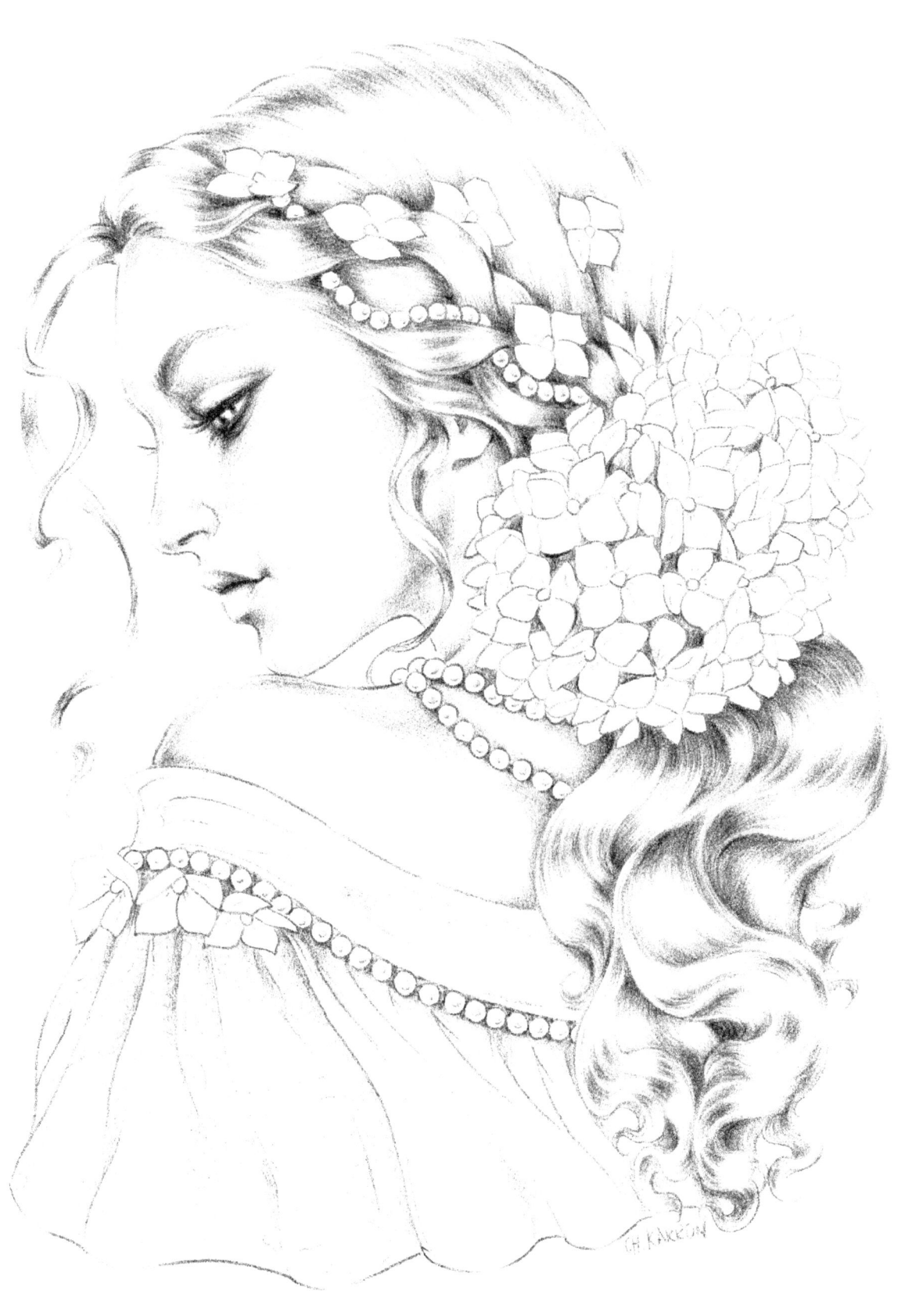

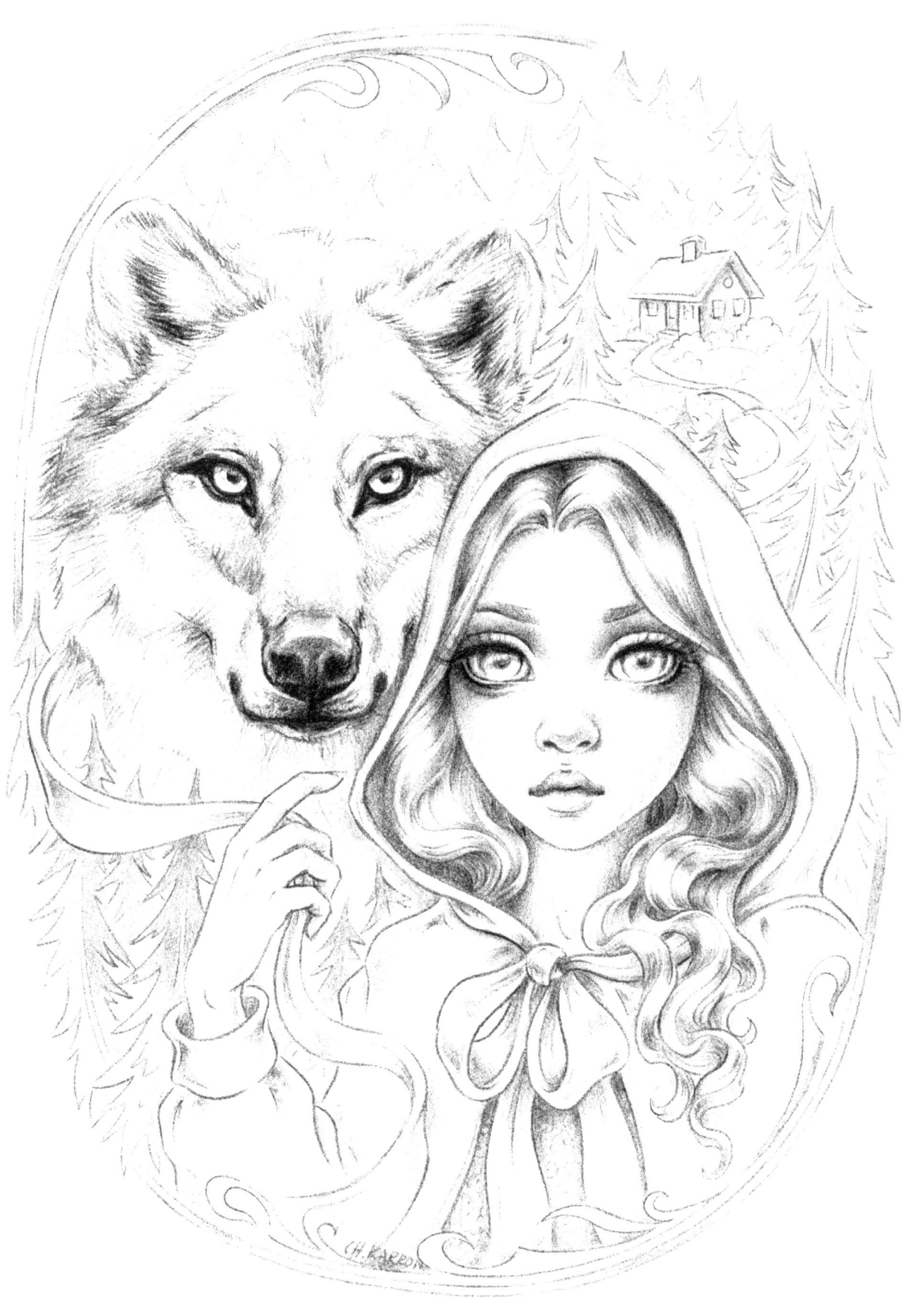

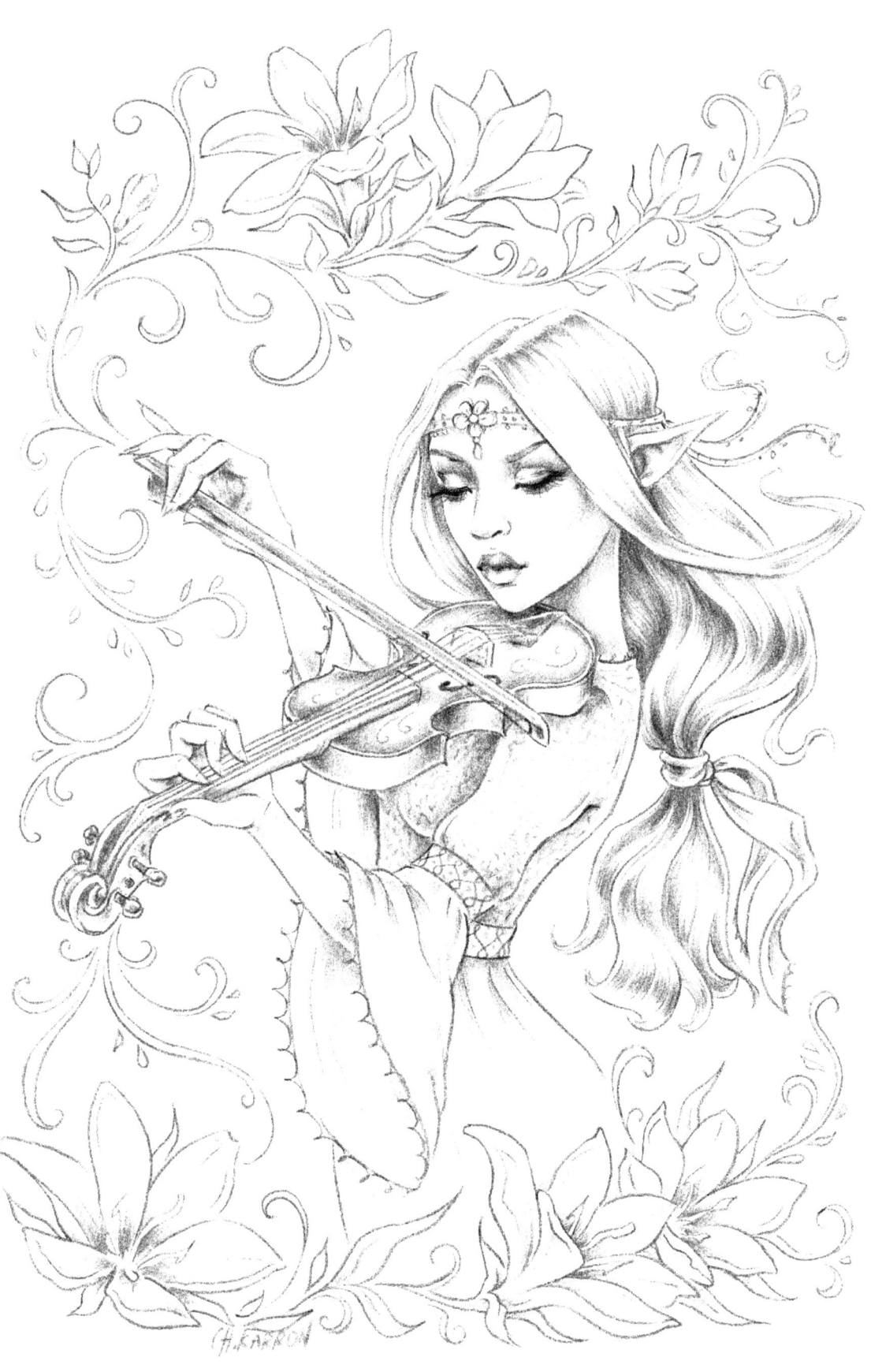

Fairy and Fantasy 2 © Christine Karron   Summer Night Fiddler

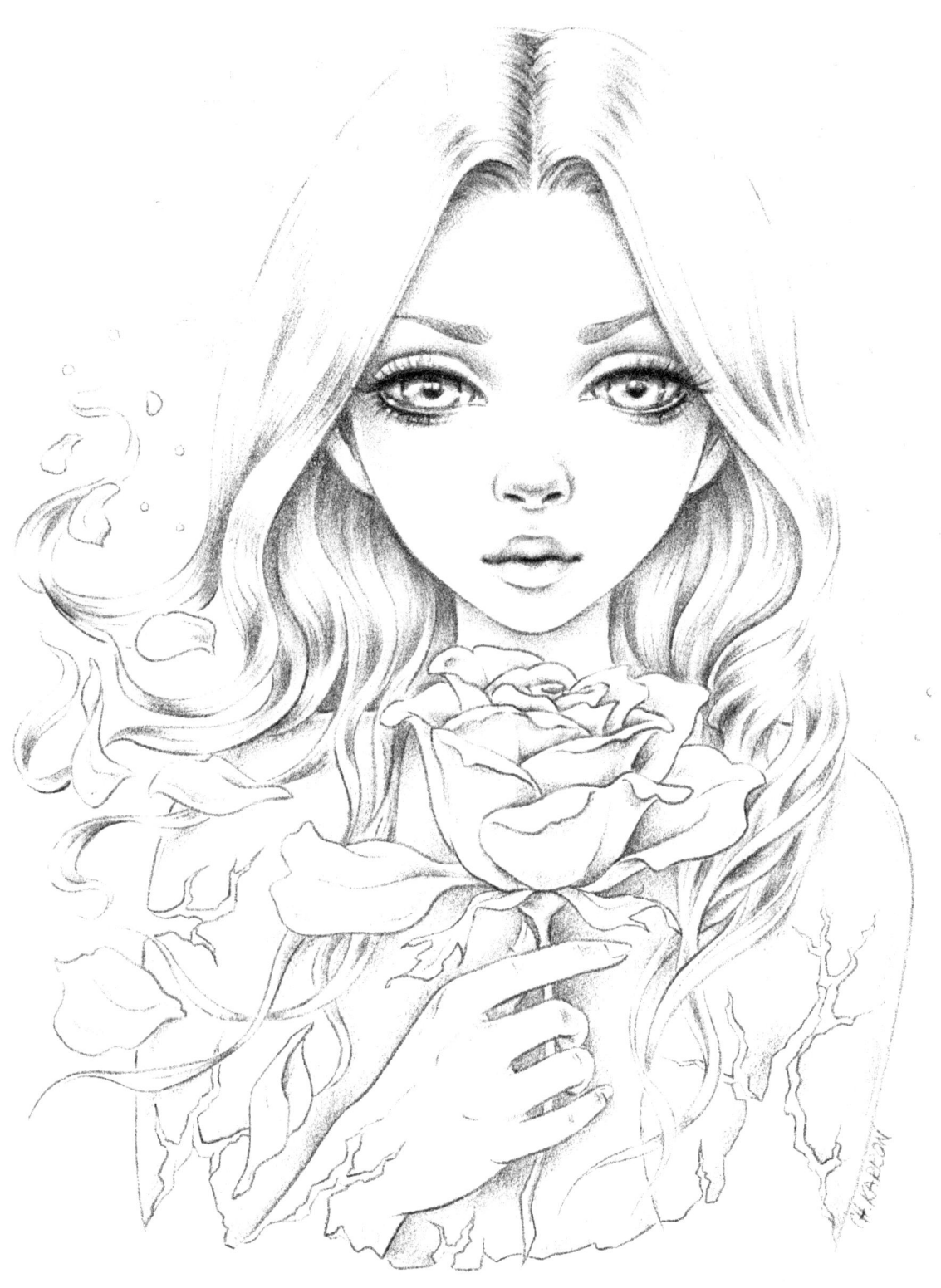

Fairy and Fantasy 2 © Christine Karron — Transience

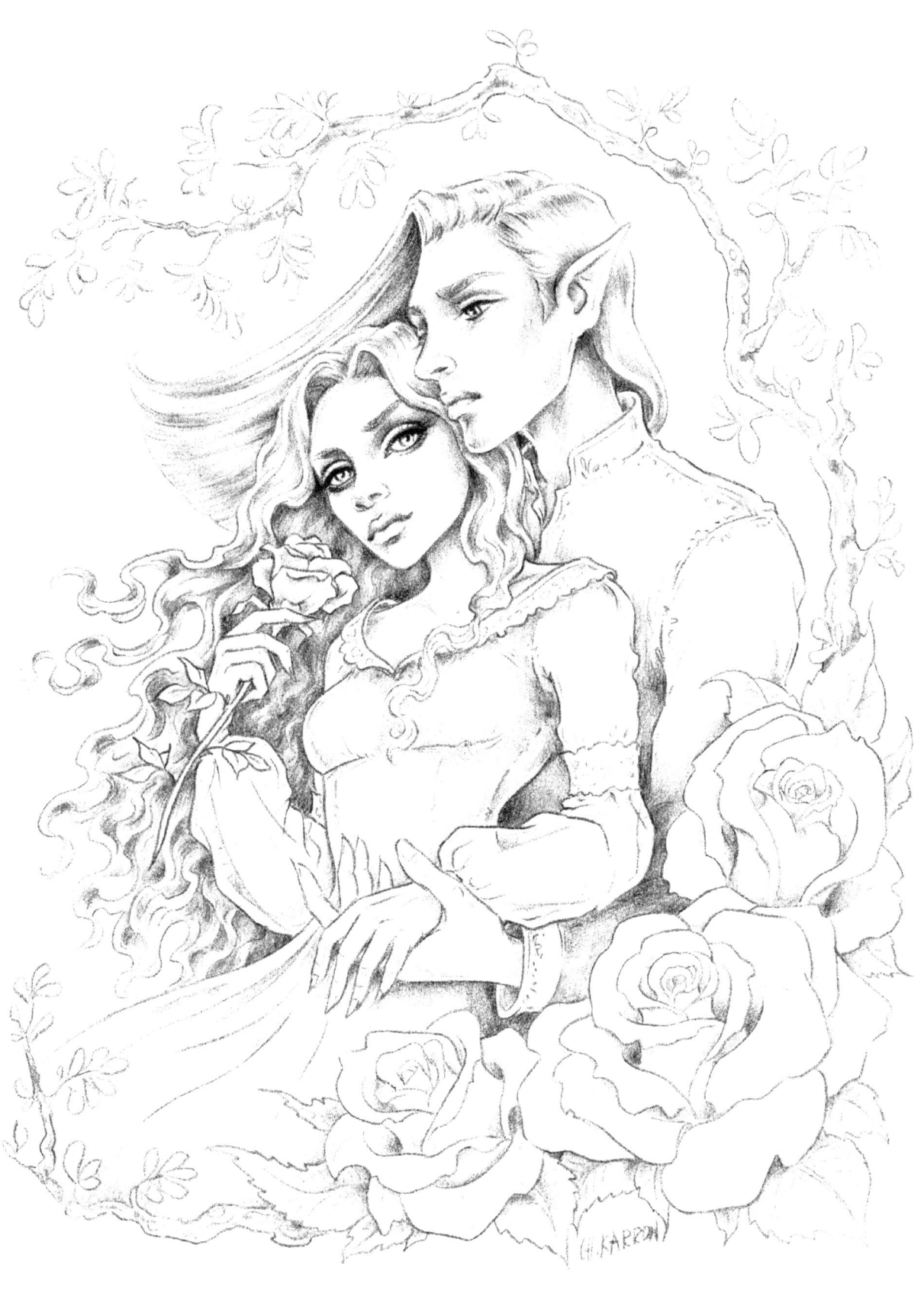

Fairy and Fantasy 2 © Christine Karron

Beloved

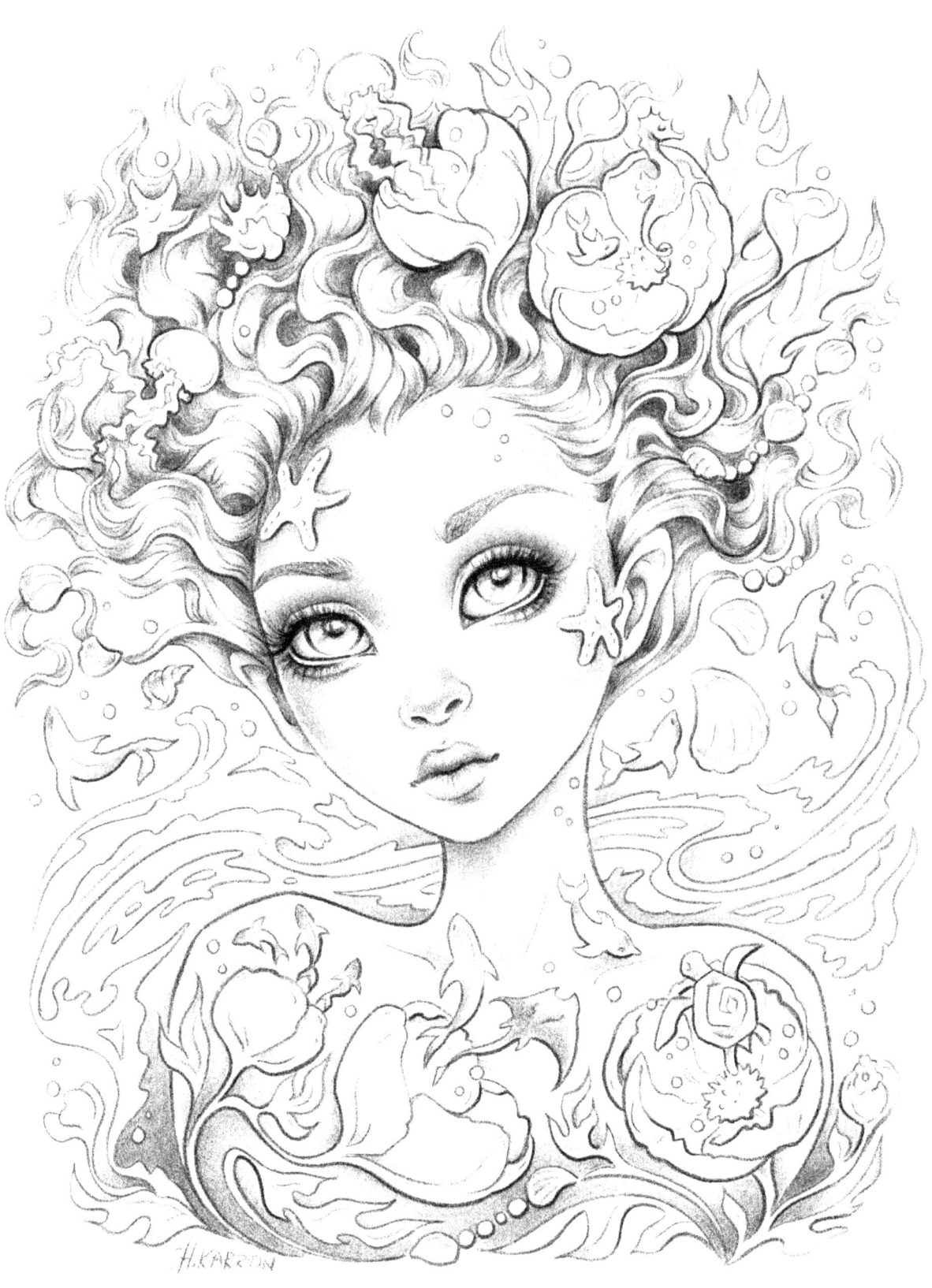

Fairy and Fantasy 2 © Christine Karron
Ocean Eyes

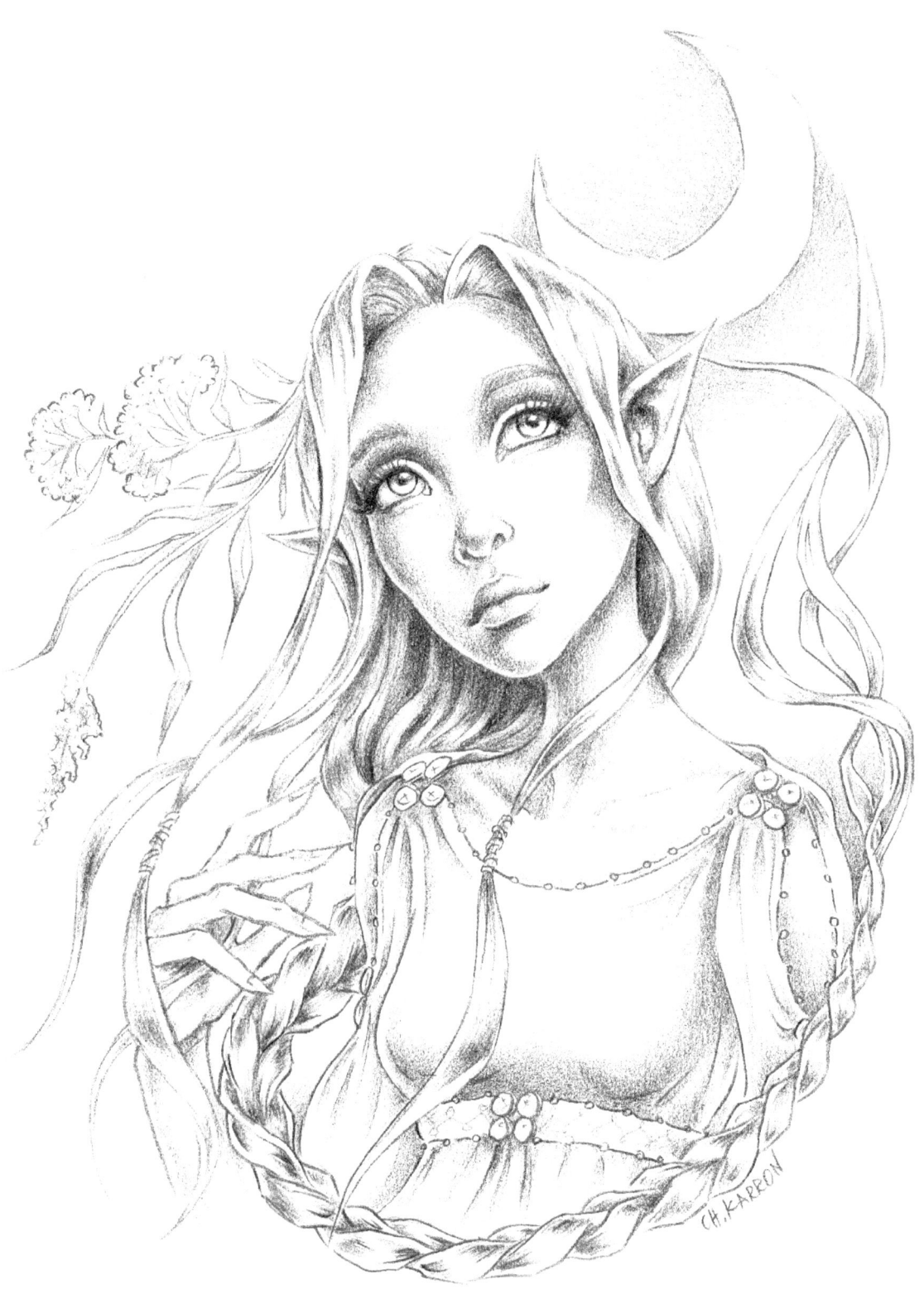

Midnight Enchantress

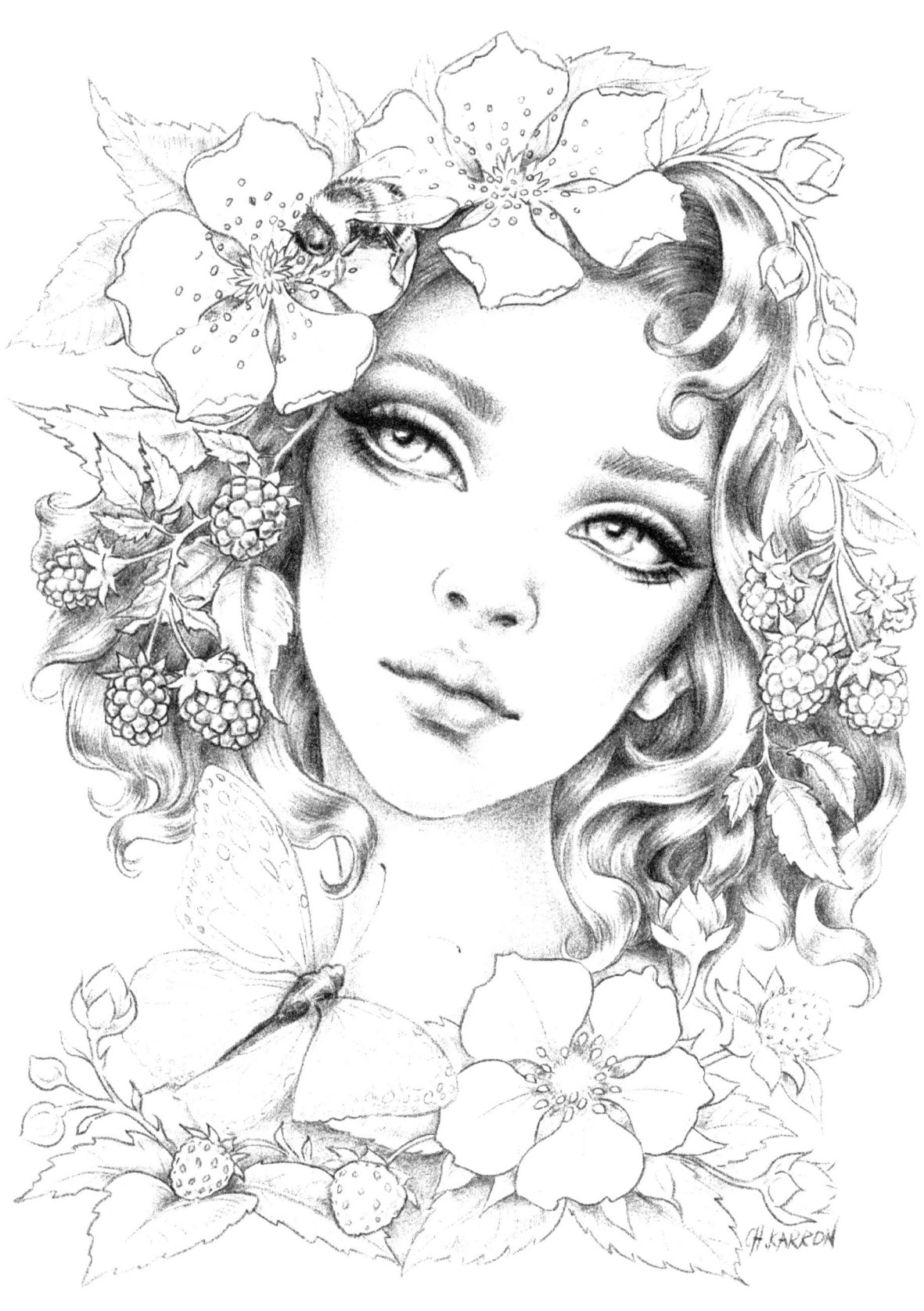

Fairy and Fantasy 2 © Christine Karron　　　　　　　　　　　　　　　　　Wildberry Bloom

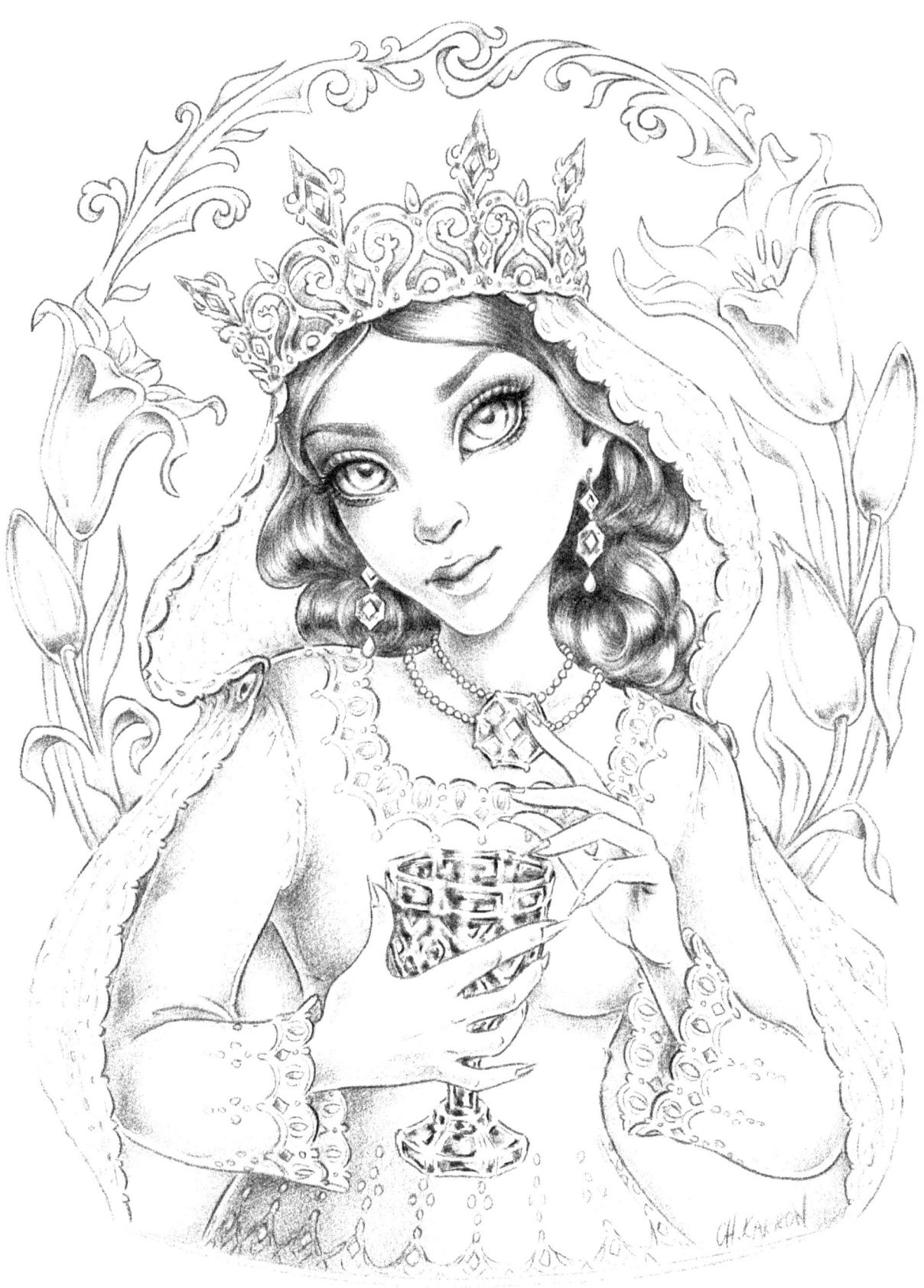

Fairy and Fantasy 2 © Christine Karron

Queen's Chalice

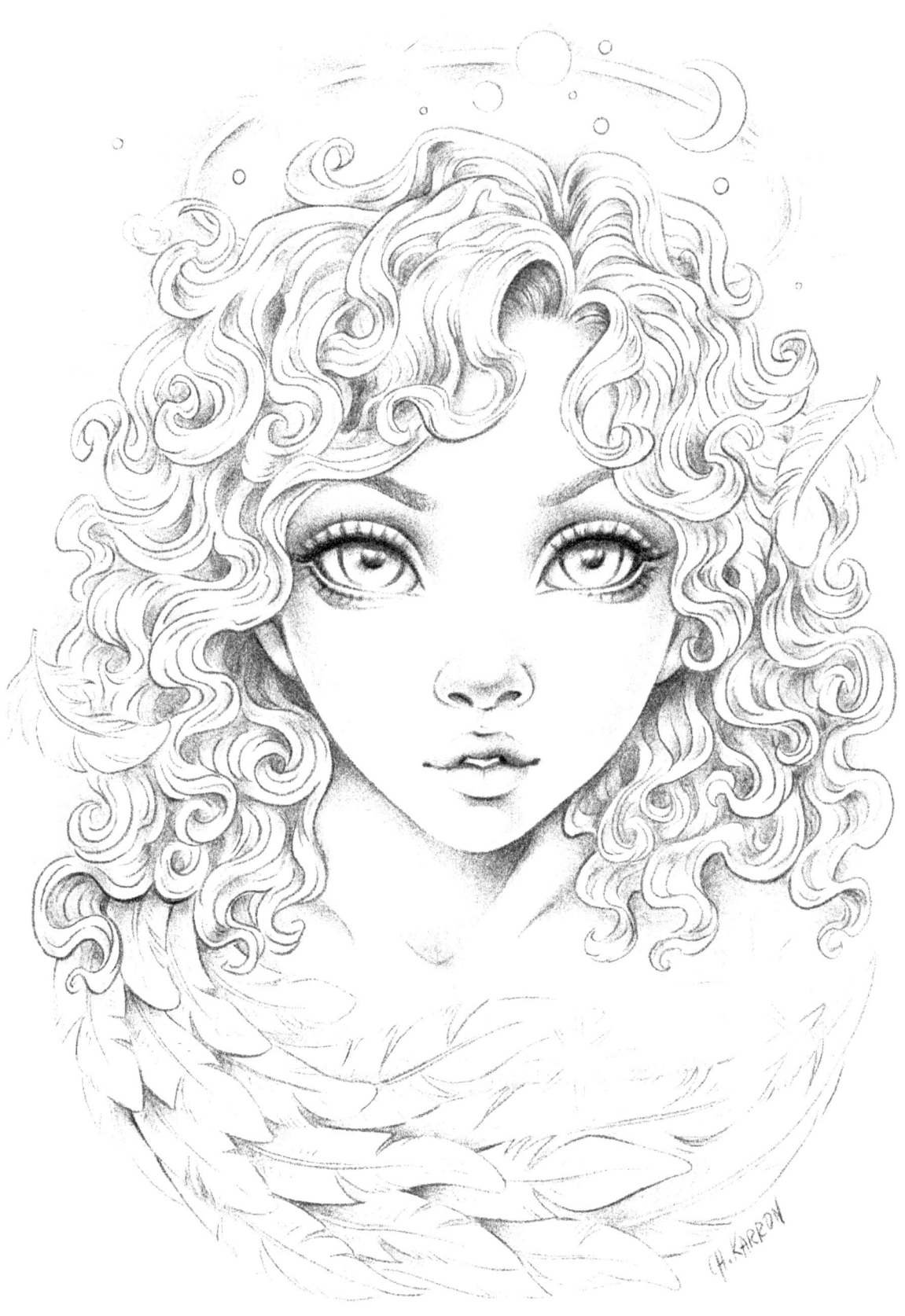

Fairy and Fantasy 2 © Christine Karron

Angel Eyes

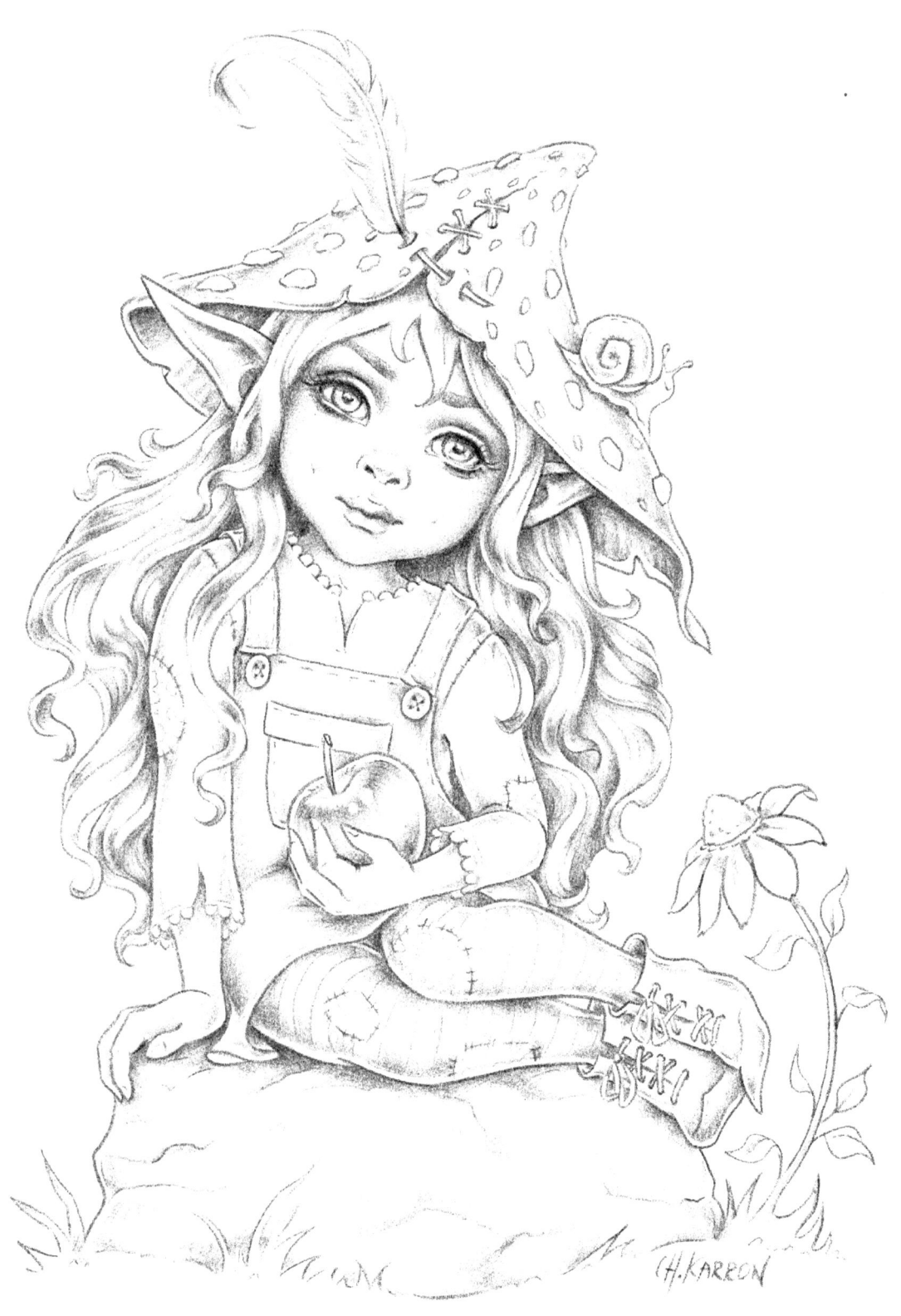

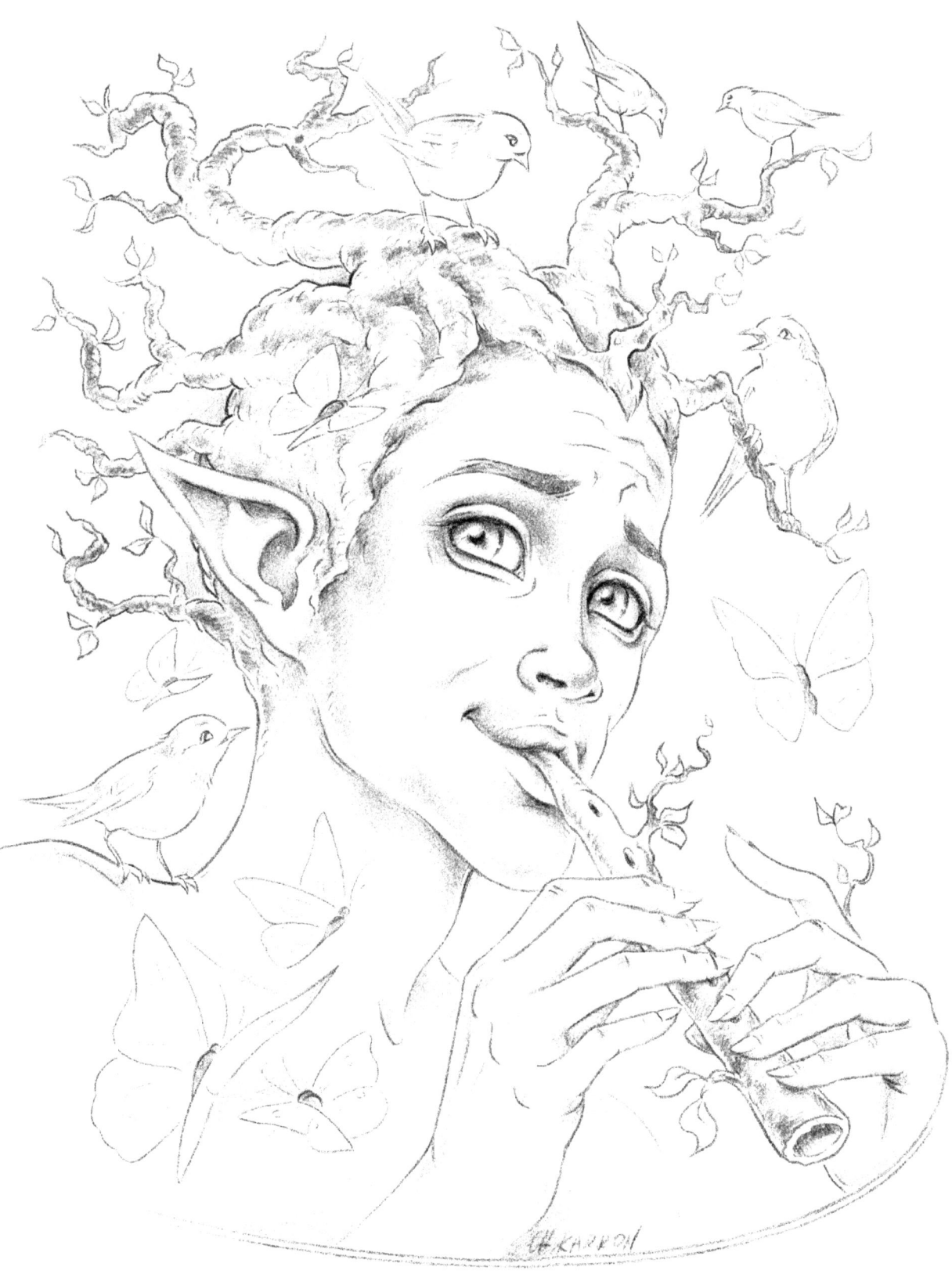

Fairy and Fantasy 2 © Christine Karron Forest Song

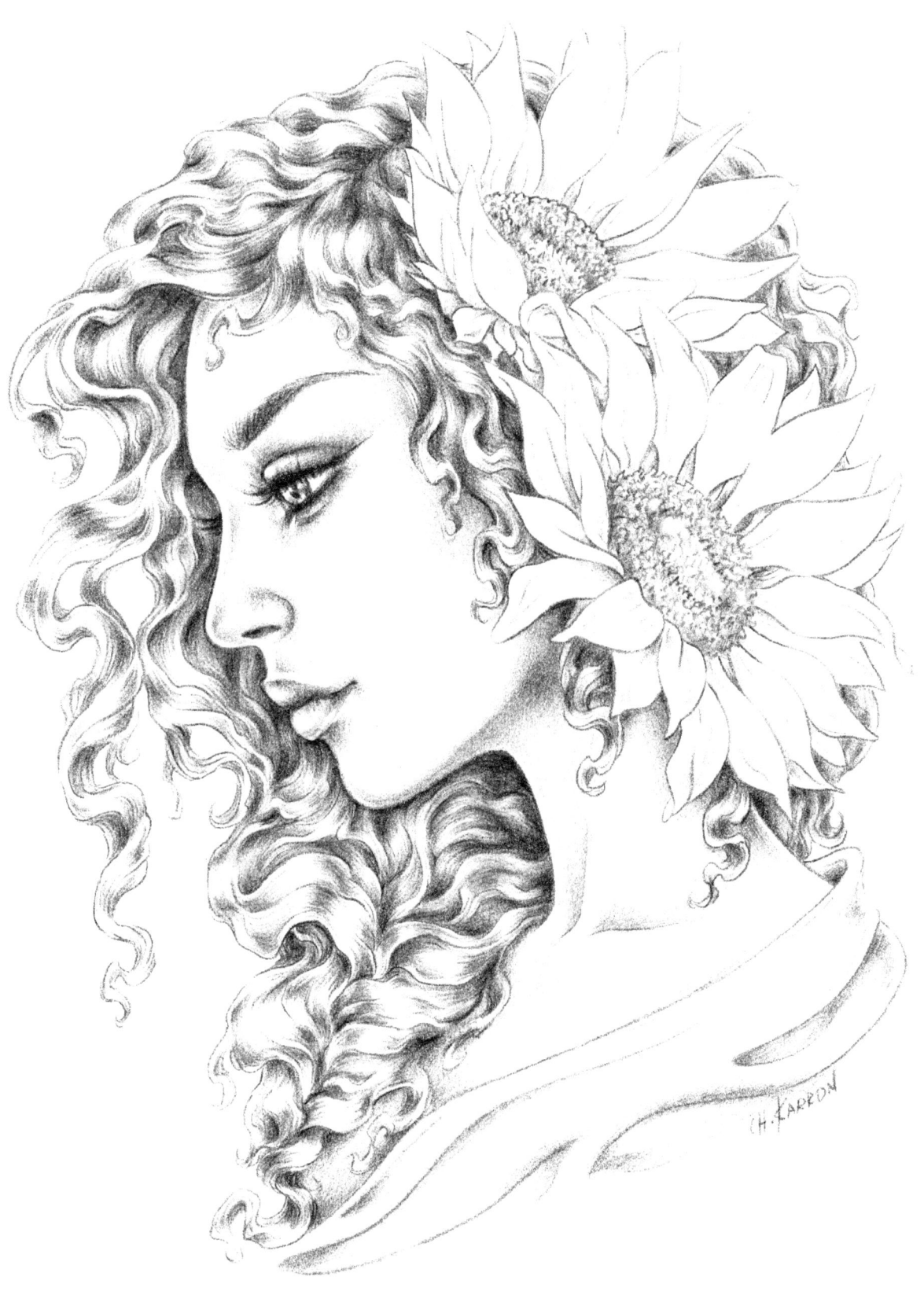

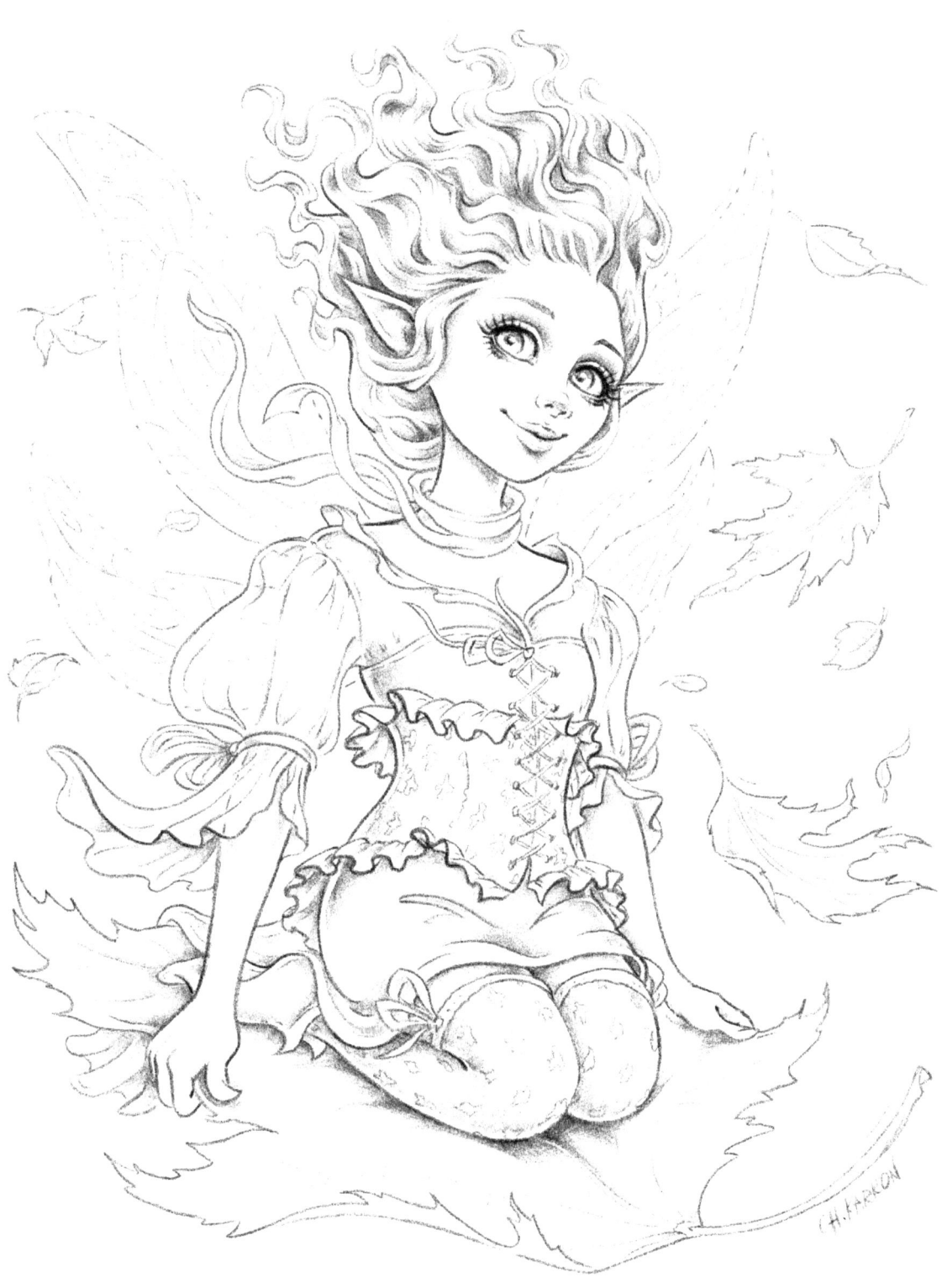

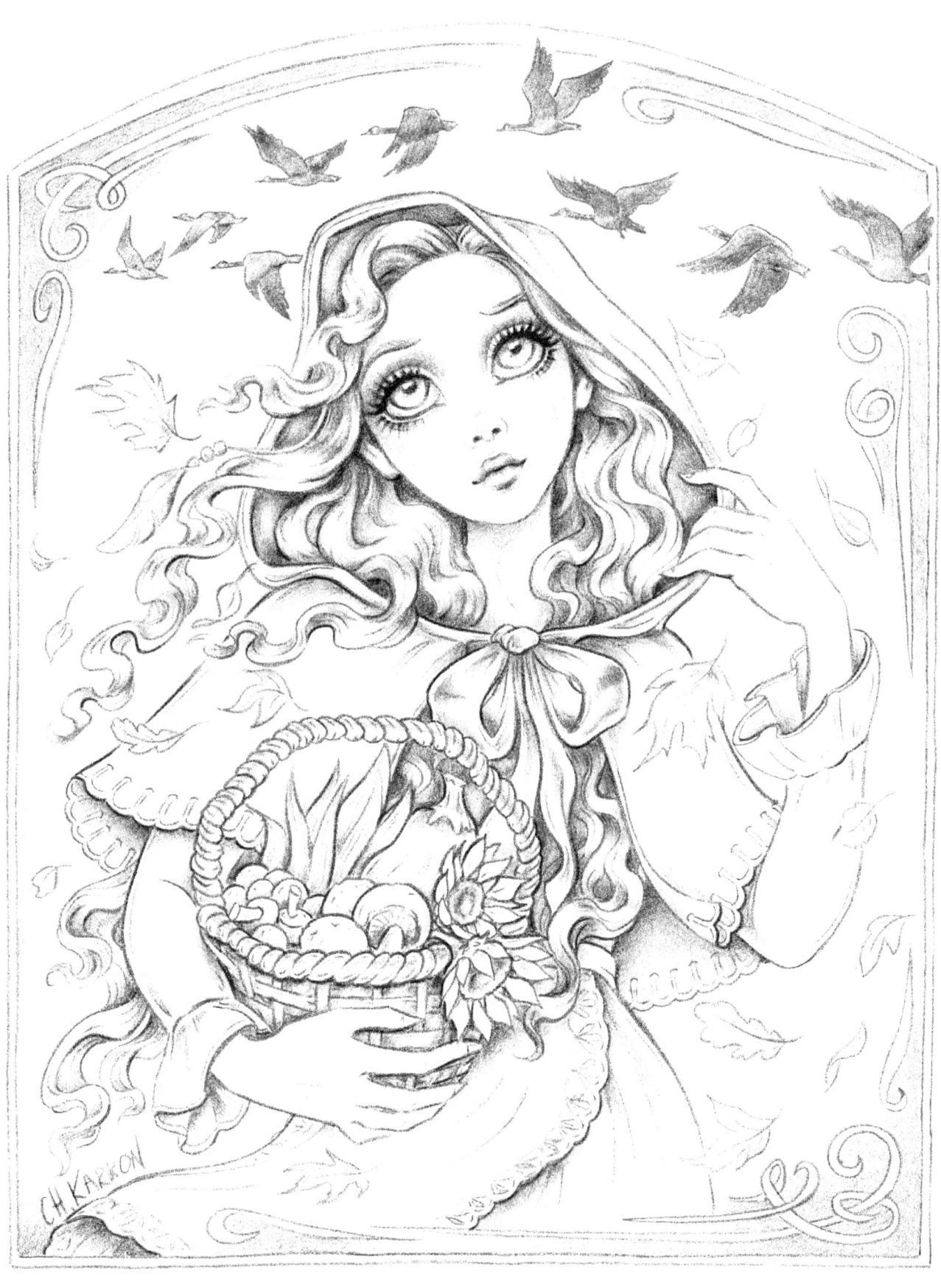

Fairy and Fantasy 2 © Christine Karron

Last Harvest

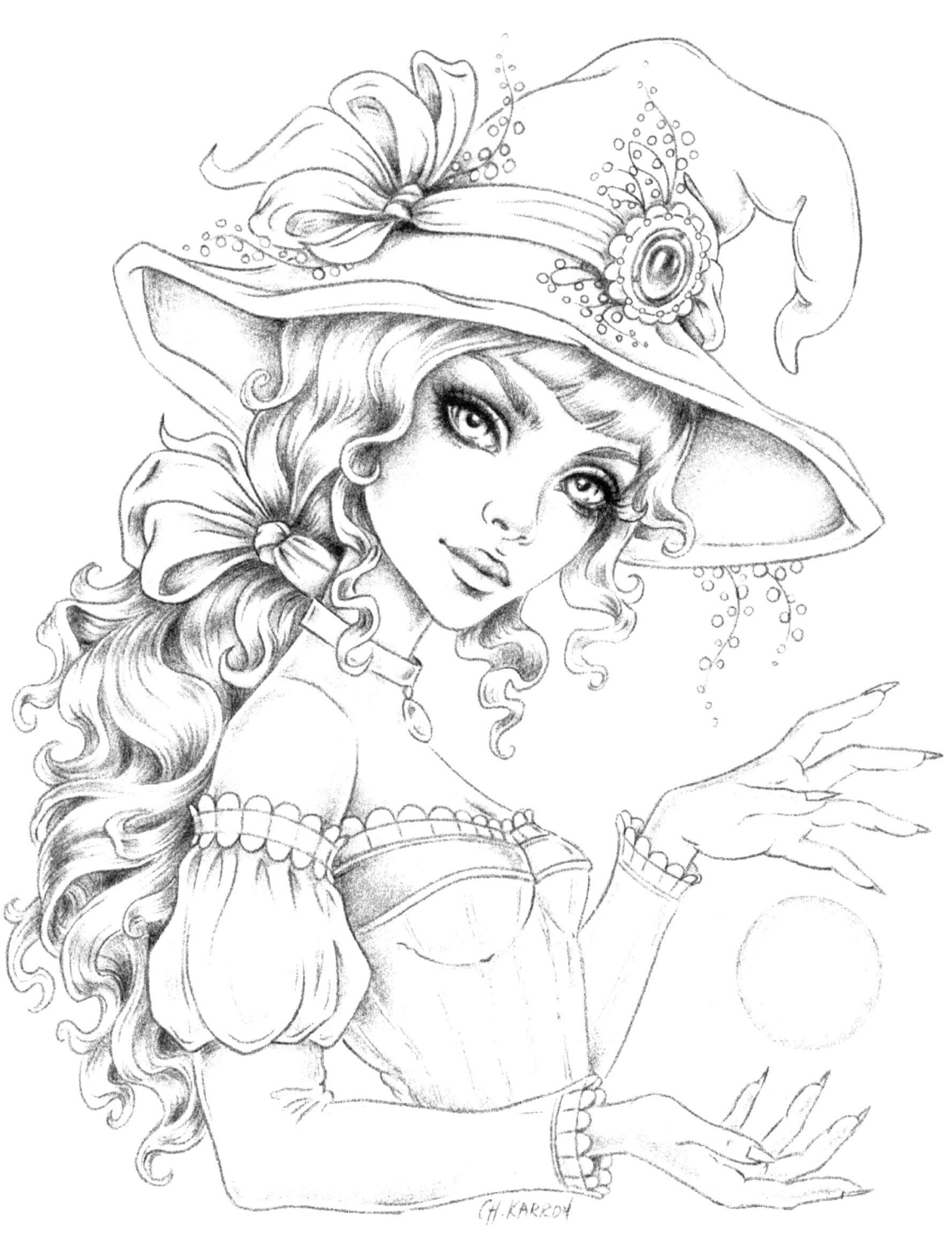

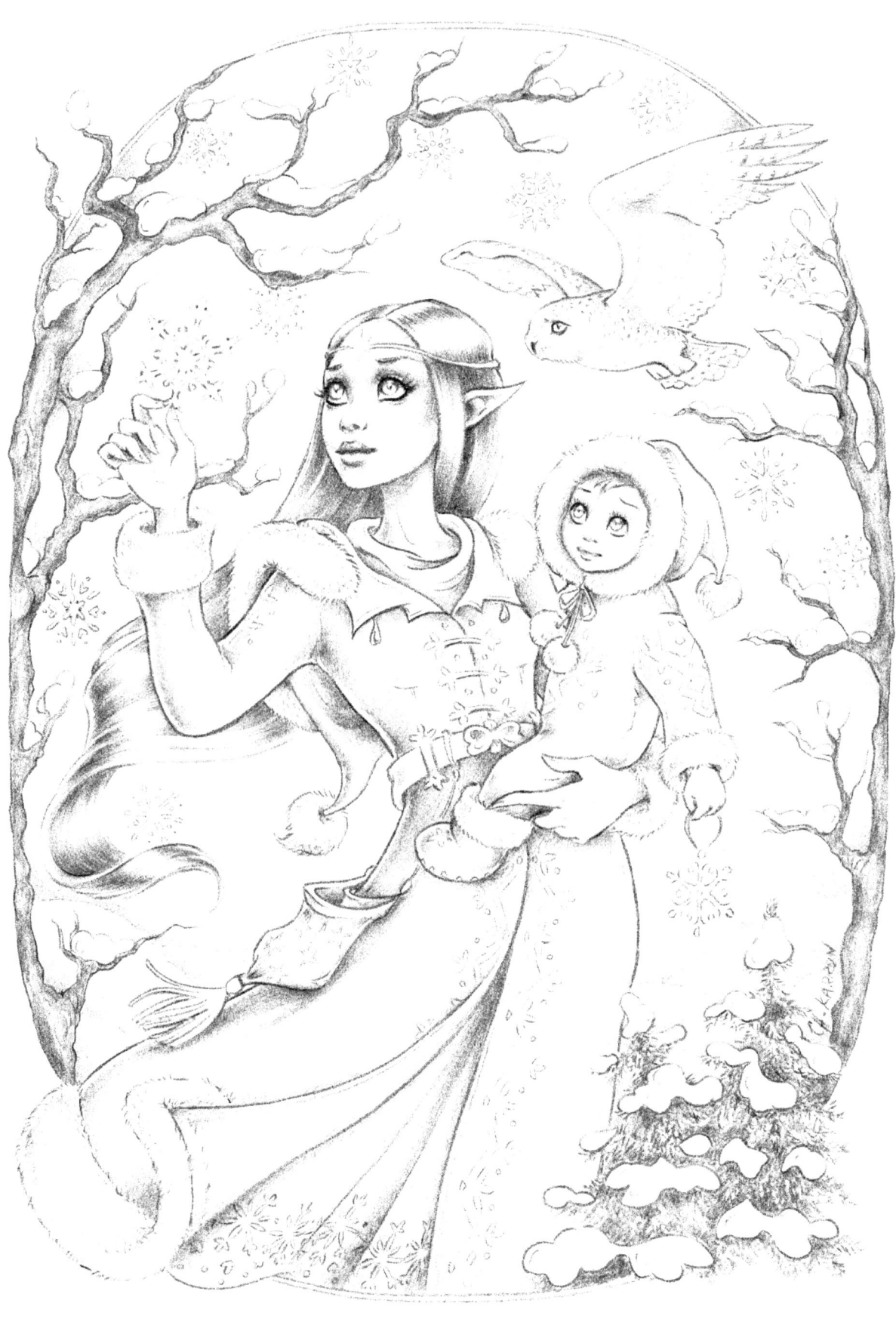

Small Wonders

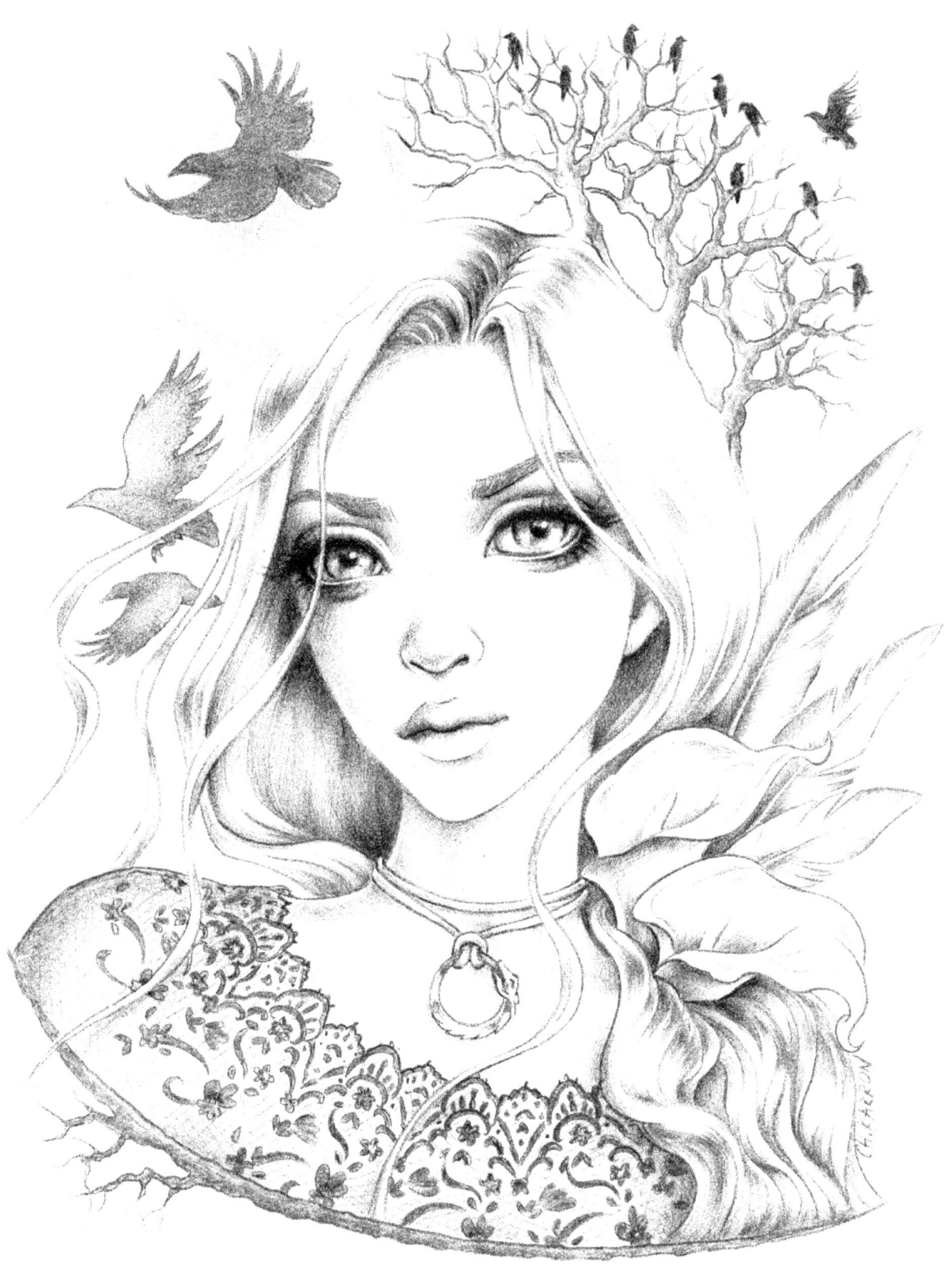

Fairy and Fantasy 2 © Christine Karron

Dark Eyes

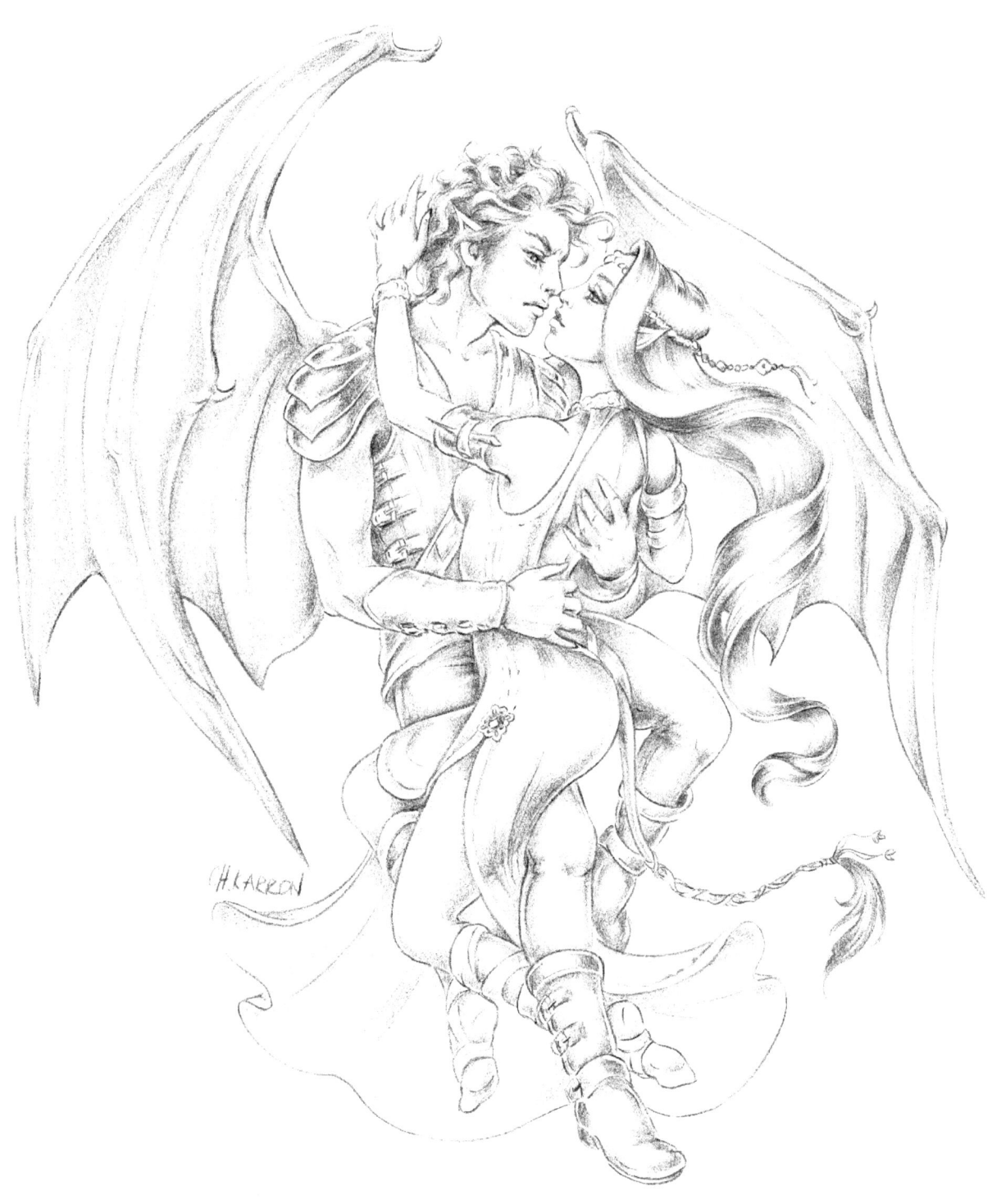

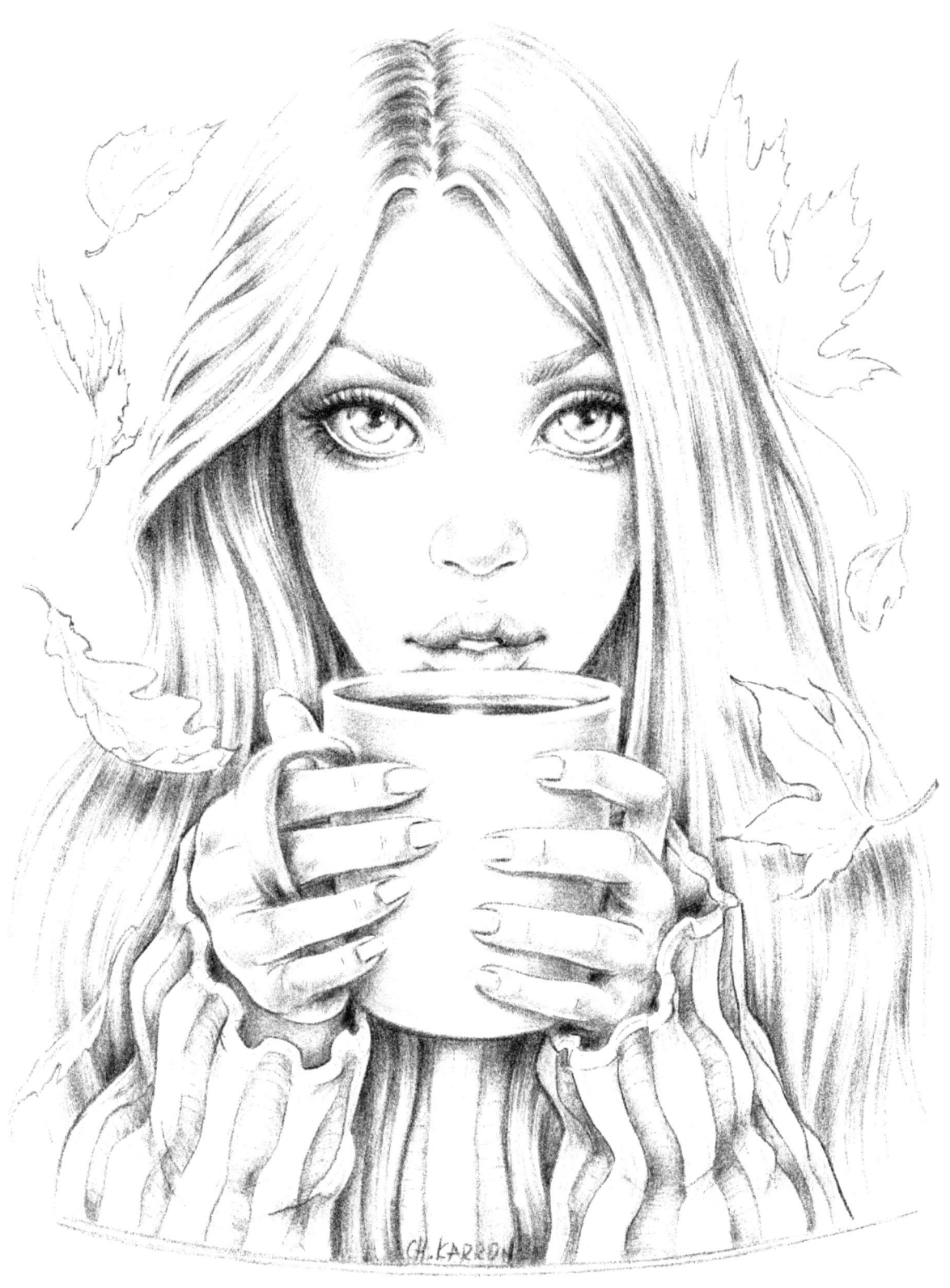

Fairy and Fantasy 2 © Christine Karron — Cup Of Warmth

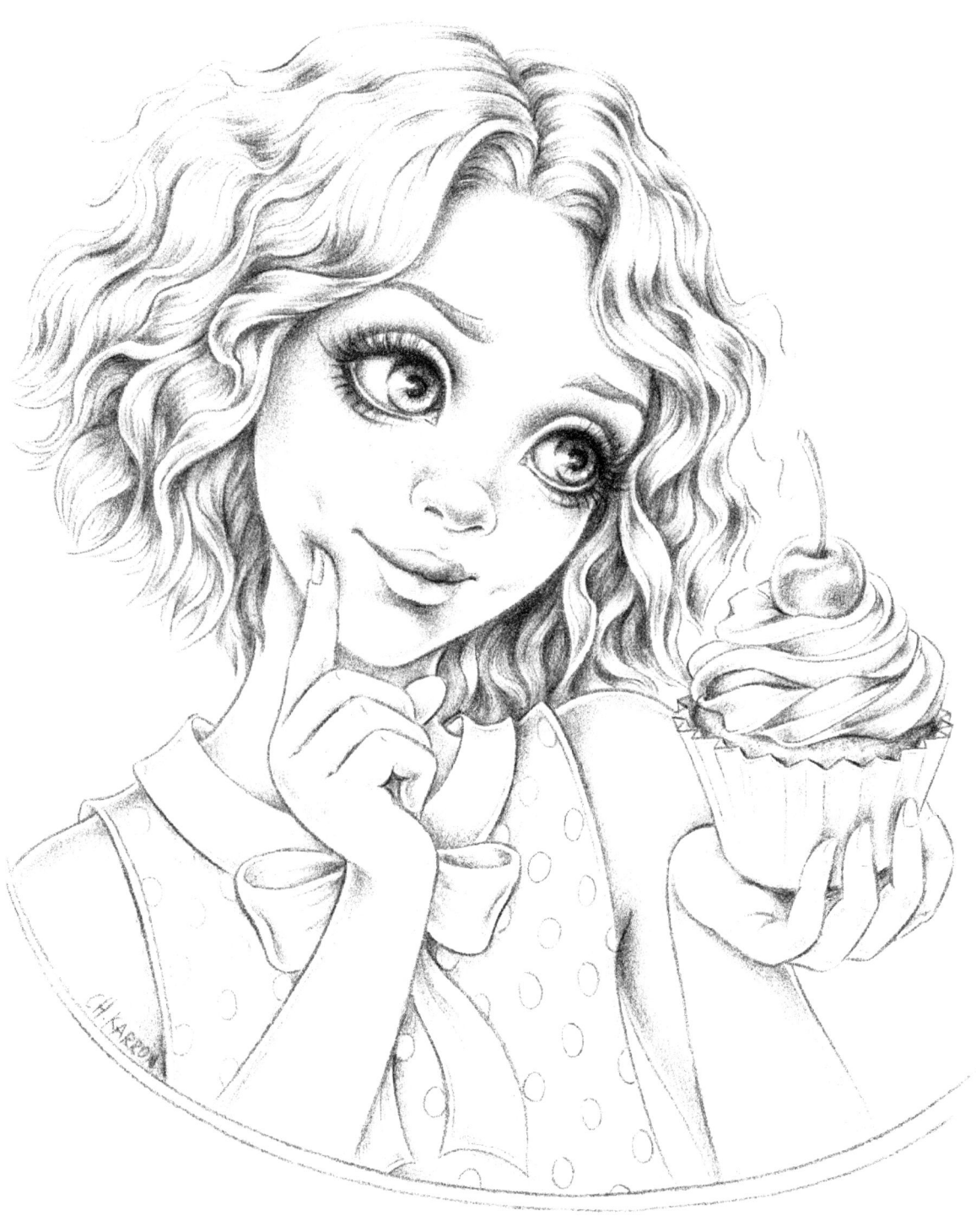

Fairy and Fantasy 2 © Christine Karron   Sweet Temptation

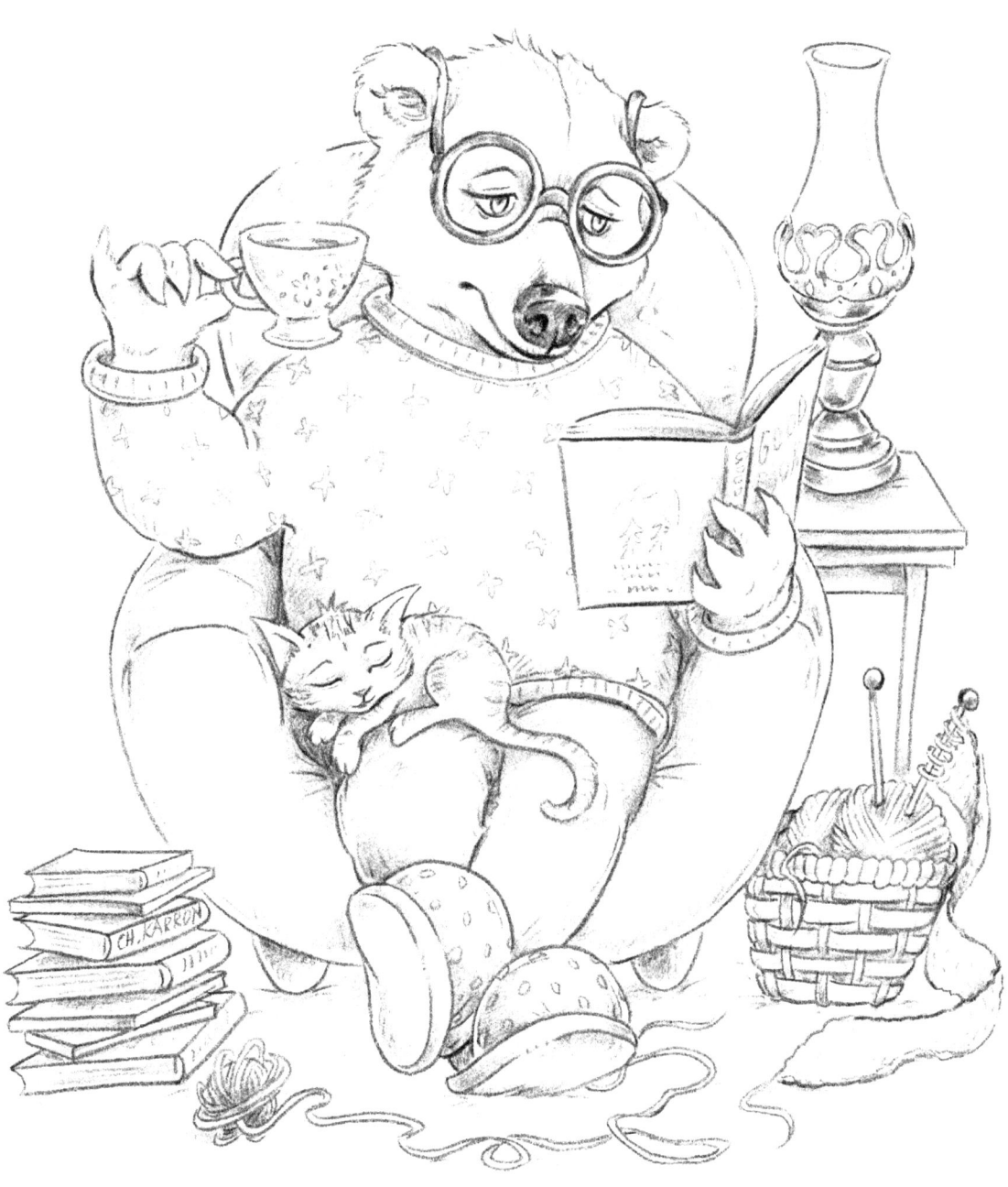

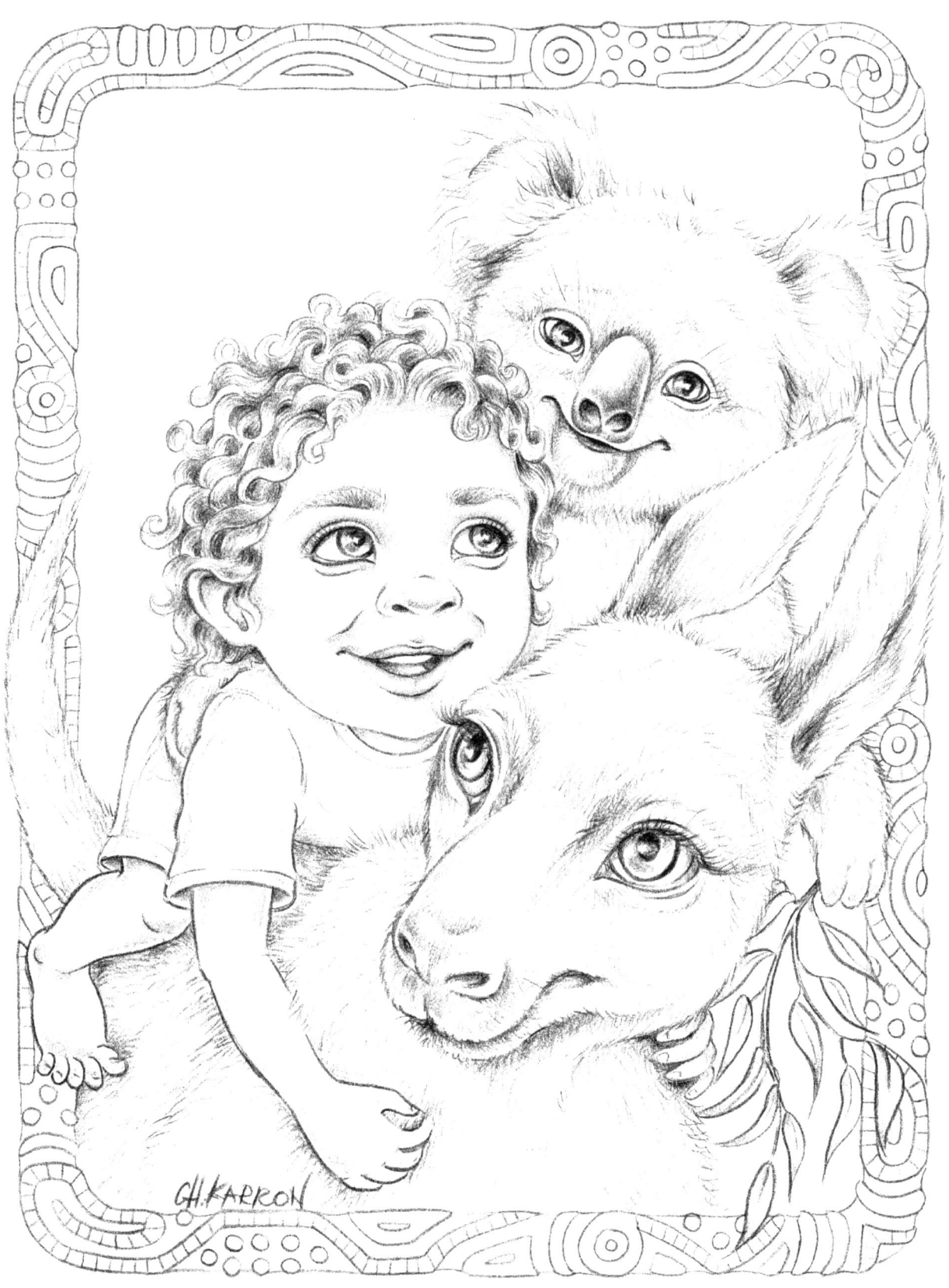

Fairy and Fantasy 2 © Christine Karron — Australia

Also available:

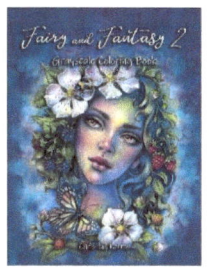 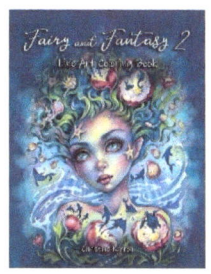 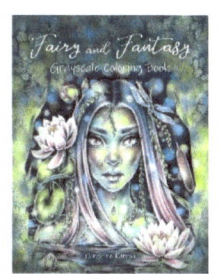 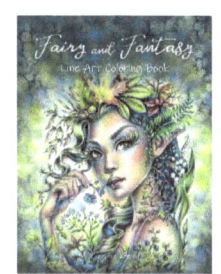 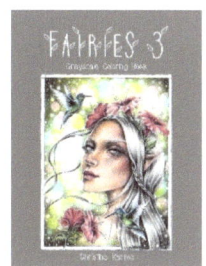

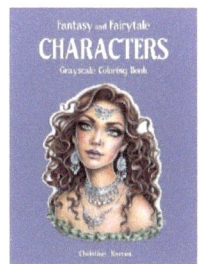 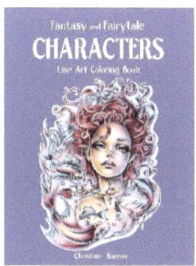 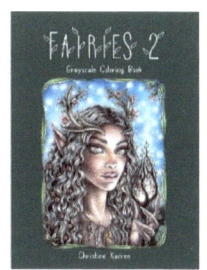 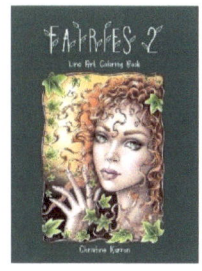 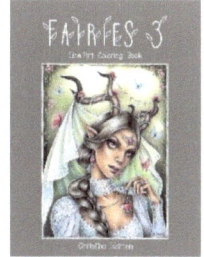

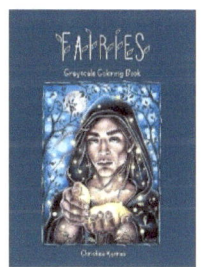 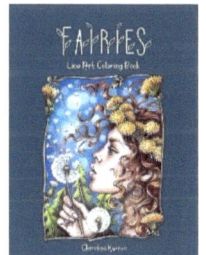 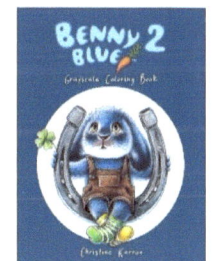 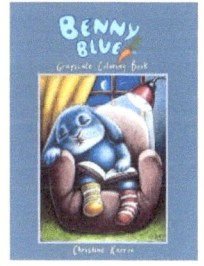 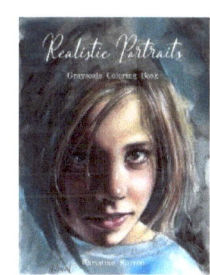

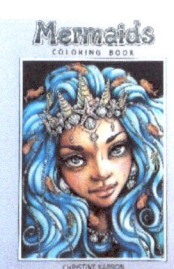 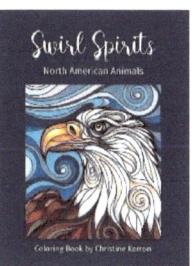

***

Christine Karron is an artist and children's book illustrator based in Alberta, Canada. Working as a freelance artist for 20 years, her artwork has been sold worldwide and includes several self-published coloring books. Christine loves to create fantasy illustrations and characters with a whimsical and narrative touch primarily using watercolor, colored pencils and ink pens/markers on paper.

Facebook:
Christine Karron Art and illustration

Facebook coloring group:
Christine Karron Coloring Collection Fan Group

Instagram: @chkarron

YouTube: Christine Karron

Etsy shop: Christine Karron
Printable digital coloring page downloads

If sharing colored images online, please credit the artist Christine Karron. You can use hashtags #christinekarron and/or #chkarron
Please DO NOT share or post uncolored versions of the images from this book on Facebook, Pinterest or any other sharing sites online.

www.chkarron.com

www.ingramcontent.com/pod-product-compliance
Lightning Source LLC
Chambersburg PA
CBHW051210220526
45473CB00003B/974